Woman, DO YOU FEEL UNWORTHY?

Sue Doble-Dumoulin

ISBN 979-8-89130-042-2 (paperback)
ISBN 979-8-89130-043-9 (digital)

Christian Faith Publishing
832 Park Avenue
Meadville, PA 16335
www.christianfaithpublishing.com

Scripture references will be from the King James Bible.

Printed in the United States of America

Woman, Do You Feel Unworthy? was written from a heart that probably understood every woman in the Bible. It comes from learning to understand who I was and how life shaped me in the wrong way. It went from seeing myself as a broken woman to seeing the God that loves and adores me did not want me to stay in that place. He comes to set the captives free, and I am free indeed. I learned through His word how He sees me. Then by His grace, I learned to speak those words over me till I knew that I knew I was that beautifully, wonderfully made woman whom God truly adores and finds no fault in me.

Introduction

Do you feel you could never be good enough for God's love, blessings, and forgiveness?

Do you live under condemnation for your past choices?

Do you feel helpless and hopeless because of those past or present sins?

I, too, have felt this way at one time or the other in my past.

God, however, wanted me to see I am no different from any other woman we find in the Bible. He said He comes to set the captives free.

"Have I also looked after Him that seeth me?" (Genesis 16:13).

God is El Roi, Hebrew for "You are the God who sees."

As we explore the women of the scriptures, knowing that El Roi saw these women also, loved them, forgave them, and, yes, blessed them. Then He is also the God that can and will do this for you today.

The Bible shows us in so many ways through various women that God's design is to save us and, yes, bless us. We will see throughout the scripture that women were the same in many ways as we are today. These women were married, widowed, single, prostitutes, prophetesses, and Queens. They were abused, loved, wealthy, poor, plain-looking, and beautiful. Young and old alike, their lives are parallel to ours.

Women have had the same problems throughout the generations. Women are sometimes broken, barren, jealous, or gentle to hard in spirit, wise or foolish—women of different races and cultures.

Who were the women of the scripture days? Are we anywhere near these women of old today? Did these women, many God-fearing women, ever make mistakes that sometimes come at a high cost? Did they ever lie, steal, connive, hate, be mean and spiteful, or unfaithful? What did God think of these women?

My goal is not for you women to see that doing wrong is okay. It is for you to see that we are free from condemnation. We are already forgiven.

We are the same as the first women of the Bible. We make mistakes or do some pretty bad things at times. With all of what took place, God never withholds His love towards us. He sent His son to set us free.

Chapter 1

LET US LOOK AT THE first woman of the scriptures. Her name was Eve. You can bet that God made this woman one good-looking babe. Adam probably went, "Wohh, oh man." God made her from the rib of Adam.

We are in a far more disorganized lifestyle than Eve, dear sisters. Look a bit at her life. No condemnation; everything around her was pure and clean. She had a perfect marriage. She had a true union with God. The animals had peace with one another. There was beauty and peace in more ways than we could comprehend.

Dear sisters, she still messed up. What is up with that? Here comes our free will, and here comes trouble.

"And the Lord God caused a deep sleep to fall upon Adam, and he slept: and He took one of his ribs, and closed up the flesh instead thereof" (Genesis 2:21–22).

And the rib which the Lord God had taken from man, made He a woman and brought her unto the man.

"Now the serpent was more subtle than any beast of the field which the Lord had made. And he said onto the woman, Yea, hath God said. Ye shall eat from every tree of the garden?" (Genesis 3:1).

What was she talking to a serpent for anyway? She knew it wasn't God. If she didn't know right at first, she had to have known after the first question.

When Eve stopped to listen to something that was contrary to what God Himself said, she set herself and Adam up for trouble. It would appear Eve stopped to listen to someone who would tell her that God didn't really know what He was talking about.

What! God's word isn't good enough for us? We think we can get our answer from a different source!

Oh, how often we do this! Then we pass it along if we can. Why do we do this? Maybe it is because it feels good or sounds inviting, to say the least.

"And when the woman saw that the tree was good for food, and that it was pleasant to the eyes, and a tree to be desired to make one wise, she took of the fruit thereof, and did eat" (Genesis 3:6).

Was Adam right there from the start? In the same sentence, it says; and also gave to her husband with her; and he did eat.

Did she bat those baby blues or maybe pucker those full ruby red lips and say (come on, honey, it tastes so good, just a little bit, I just know you'll like it!).

Watch how one act of disobedience starts rolling downhill. God called them up on the carpet for this act of disobedience.

"And the man said, the woman who thou gavest to be with me, she gave me of the tree, and I did eat it" (Genesis 3:12).

Nothing like passing the buck and blaming it on someone else; putting the blame on God is downright bold and also true full-blown rebellion.

And God said to the woman, what is this that thou hast done? And the woman said, the serpent beguiled me, and I did eat.

In today's world, it would go something like this. It's your fault, God; after all, you're the one that gave her to me in the first place. It's her fault, too; she wanted me to try it out.

Honestly, would we ever do something like this? We do it all the time if we are honest with ourselves. We, as humans, do not want to stand up and be accountable for our sins without taking someone down with us most of the time.

What happened to the first couple? The couple was then punished, as is told in Genesis 3:23–24. Yet, in the next chapter, you can see that God blessed Eve with children. Wow, the first woman of the scriptures to give birth. By the way, as a point of interest, that was the start of the belly button.

Let us look a little bit more at this new mom. After her rebellion against the Lord, one might think she was going to make sure her children knew the consequences of going against God. Cain and Abel could both learn from their mom's knowledge.

Can you hear her saying? "Look, boys, I've told you what it was like in the garden before I disobeyed God, don't go down that same path as your dad and I did. Learn from our mistakes."

How many moms have tried to raise their kids right and still have one or two that will not yield to God? Me too; I am one of those mothers.

Out of the first two kids on earth, we have one that is greedy with God. Jealous of his brother and then a murderer, he bumps his brother off because of the jealousy. How's that for odds? Here we have two kids, with one being a bad seed.

Here comes condemnation for the parents. Where did I go wrong? If I had only been a better mom or dad, if I, if I. You grab the apple tree branch and give yourselves a good whipping with it. Maybe time after time, year after year, you shed tears and agonize over your failures. We do not let grace abound. We may not even know what grace really is, even if we are Christians.

Chapter 2

How about that Sarai girl? Abram took this beauty for his wife. She was his half-sister. Uck, in those days, this was acceptable with needing to populate the earth. What kind of woman was this breathtaking beauty?

We do know in Genesis 11:30 that Sarai was incapable of having children. Scripture says, now Sarai, Abram's wife, bares him no children.

As many married couples still do today, they packed up and left their hometown to start a new life in another district. They were traveling along, and they came upon the Egyptians. Abram became a scaredy cat and thought he might get bumped off if they knew he was Sarai's husband.

She must have been a real knockout in her day. What happens is dear old hubby tells her to lie and say she is his sister! Kind of the truth, don't you think? What has been brought to my attention in this story is that this couple loved the Lord and had a servant's heart. What did Abram say? He said to lie. Okay, hubby, but lie to whom exactly? Why Pharaoh himself, my love.

You just told your wife to lie to the big man of the country. What might happen out of that? Sarai told a lie, and God punished Pharaoh and his house with great plagues. Yep, someone other than yourself got hurt by your lie. Someone you never knew before personally got hurt. The lie didn't do any damage to Abram and Sarai.

How many times in life do our lies hurt someone else more than it hurts us? In the long run, those lies do have a devastating effect on us; they separate us from our union with God and destroy relationships with family and friends. It can go further in as much as other people will not try to get to know you because they know what you have done.

You would think that this lovely couple would learn from past mistakes. Do we, my dear ladies, keep making the same mistakes? Do we sometimes need a few hard lessons?

Let's get back to the lovely couple. Did they continue to do things that would dishonor God? Did they continue to lie? Genesis 20:2–3 says, "And Abraham and his wife Sarah (notice God gave them new names by this time) she is my sister: and Abimelech, king of Gerar, sent and took Sarah."

Goodness me, the same old lie, and this time to the king who would be sleeping with her. Are they going to get found out for this big whopper?

Verse 3, but God came to Abimelech in a dream at night, and said to him, Behold thou art a dead man, for the woman which thou hast taken: she is a man's wife.

Verse 4, But Abimelech had not come near her: and he said: Lord wilt thou also slay a righteous nation?

Scripture goes on to say that Abraham told not the truth about his relationship with Sarah. Also, God knew the king's heart to be of integrity, so he caused him not to sin. That was a break; there could have been hard times for everyone because of this lie. I would suggest you read all of chapter 20; Abraham confesses his lied to the king and gets money and animals from the king just so he can get them out of his sight. Has someone ever given you something to get rid of you? Did you ever gain from a sin you committed? What is the chance of that? This reward could be a reminder of your sin every time you look at it. How much fun is that? After Jesus shed His blood and was whipped in an inch of His life, we now live under grace.

Abraham then prayed to God for Abimelech, his wife, and his maidservants, and they bore children. Look closely at the consequences, dear ladies. The sin of Abraham and Sarah caused other wombs to be closed up.

Abraham, not once but twice, chose to justify his lie by twisting the truth. What really struck me about all this is Abraham's talk with God, and his honesty, repentance, and forgiveness are evident in the scriptures, for grace abounded, and there were blessings that came from it. We all want that in our lives, do we not?

Going back to the life of Sarah before she conceived, she thought she should take these matters into her own hands to get a son for her hubby. Did she think God was talking out of the wrong side of his mouth, or maybe He was a little daft? Didn't God say in chapter 12:2, "And I will make thee a great nation?"

Sarah had her handmaid sleep with the hubby, and it brought forth a son. The handmaid's name was Hagar (Hagar was one of the presents given to the lovely couple to get lost). After Hagar had the baby, she rubbed Sarah's nose into it.

Chapter 16:5 is especially important.

And Sarah said, "My wrong be upon me."

She saw she had gone ahead of God, and now she was reaping the consequences for it.

Sarah dealt harshly with Hagar, and Hagar took off. What kind of punishment did she bring upon Hagar to leave? You would think she would have been happy about it all; after all, it was her idea. Have you ever been so mad at someone or them at you that you would leave and never want to come back?

God told Hagar to go back. I bet she was scared stiff. God also told her to submit, and He would bless her for it.

Two different women, two different backgrounds, both pulling some nasties, yet the one true God came to bless them.

When it was time for Hagar and her son to leave for good, it was Abraham that finally put it into action. Yet both Ismael and Isaac came together to bury their dad when he gave up his spirit.

Chapter 3

Hagar

THIS WOMAN WAS A SLAVE to Sarah. How did she become one? The scriptures tell us that when King Abimelech gave a bootee for Abraham and Sarah to get out of town, Hagar was part of the deal. Boy, if it were me, I would be resentful. Family, friends, and her way of life were all gone. Then you become a slave of a stranger who makes you sleep with her hubby.

Hagar became a rival to Sarah. Once she became pregnant, she had a very condescending attitude toward Sarah. When this happened, Sarah had no mercy on Hagar.

Twice God intervened on Hagar's behalf. Hagar had no say in being a part of the gift to dear old Abe and his wife, nor did she have any say in what she was put through with this family she was forced into.

I don't know about you, dear ladies, but if it were me with the personality, I would have rubbed Sarah's nose in it big time. God did bless her for this with a son, and the son was given much stature.

Chapter 4

Lot's Wife

WE ARE NOW GOING TO have a peek at "Lot's Wife," starting with Genesis 19. Sodom was full of homosexuals at this time.

Two angels in human form came at this time to save a few good people. This was due to the prayers of Abraham. When the evil men of this town tried to capture the angels, Lot went and offered up his two virgin daughters. What kind of a good dad does this? What kind of an animal was dear old dad? He was willing to throw his girls to the wolves.

A smart one, I soon discovered. These corrupt men were not about to take on the girls. It was, though, a good distraction for a little while. The angels were safe.

We did not hear a word if Mommy was upset by good old dad offering up her precious girls. What we do know, though, is that God came to save that family.

What do we know about Mom? We know that she disobeyed God and turned into a pillar of salt because she looked back when God said do not look back. Why did she look back?

We wonder if we do know from chapter 19, verse 14 that Lot went and spoke unto the sons-in-law that married his daughters and said, "Up, get out of this place!" Did leaving other families there and maybe good friends cause her to look back?

It is hard to be obedient to God when he wants us to close a chapter of our lives. Nevertheless, we must submit to the Lord's will in our lives. When we do not, we suffer consequences. She paid the penalty of death at the hands of God for not doing what God told her. She stopped to look instead of marching on with God. Why does He give someone a second chance and another not? The answer lies with God and God alone. In the Old Testament, God did punish. Ladies, get it into your head and heart deep down into your spirit that was the old. Under the new covenant through the blood of Jesus, there is forgiveness of sin. When rotten stuff comes at us, we need to be well aware of the covenant promises and kick Satan to the curb. He is behind this belief making you think God is punishing you. Not so, you beautiful women.

Do you, dear ladies, stop to look at the sin you have to leave behind? Do you feel you are justified by this, or do you think it is just too hard to go forward? Do you end up paying a high price for it all? Is the disobedience worth it in the end? I think not.

Chapter 5

Rahab

Joshua 2 tells us about Rahab. Rahab was a bad woman in most people's eyes; perhaps, in today's society, she would be considered one. She was a prostitute.

In biblical times, there were two kinds of prostitutes. There was the religious type, who was at the temple of the Canaanites doing their thing, or like Rahab, who did it for a living.

The Hebrew word for this line of work is Zonah; the Greek word is porne. You can color it any color you like, but in the end, she was a prostitute. Rahab was a woman that was talked about a lot, but I am sure not over the dinner table or in high society luncheons. She had family who lived in the neighborhood, but she was on her own to support herself.

This young woman had been around the block, as the old saying goes, and she knew how to handle men. She spent time seizing them up and learned of their habits and needs.

How many of us women take time to do this for our betrothed or our husbands? If we did, our marriage would be more harmonious.

Rahab, according to scriptures, was one of the four most beautiful women in the ancient world. Then why had she become a lady of the night? She could have had nearly any man, I am sure. One can only speculate on this.

What we do know is that she had a calling on her life to help two men of God. Not just to help them but to risk her life. She could have gone down for the count if she had gotten caught. She disobeyed the king of that time to help these men. She lied when she was told to give them up, and she said they were gone already when in fact, they were hiding on the roof. She let these men down on a rope to safety. She hung out her scarlet cord for the world to see what she was as a scarlet woman, a hooky cookie; she did this that day so God's men could be free.

How many cheating men were let down the same rope? One can only imagine!

God was really more concerned with her heart. She neither was far from perfect nor was she a woman of greatness—a scarlet woman covered and cleansed by the scarlet blood, forever changed.

"She perished not with them that believe not when they received the spies with peace" (Hebrews 11:31). Rahab was clever and courageous. She was also so loved by God that she was lineage to Christ.

> Salmon the father of Boaz, whose mother was Rahab. Rahab became the grandmother of Obed, whose mother was Ruth. Jessie was the son of Obed and Jessie the father of King David. (Matthew 1:5–6)

Look at the blessings that went down the generations for the faithfulness of a woman who had a shady past.

Dear ladies, if God can take a lady of the night and use her lineage to lead directly to the king of kings, then dear heart, he has no less love for you. From a red cord on display for everyone to see, saying I get around, I am a red cord woman, to line up with the King of Glory. You go, girl! Only God can change a harlot into a hero. It does not matter who you were; it matters who you are. Dear, dear ladies, God has no less love for you. Don't ever doubt that.

Chapter 6

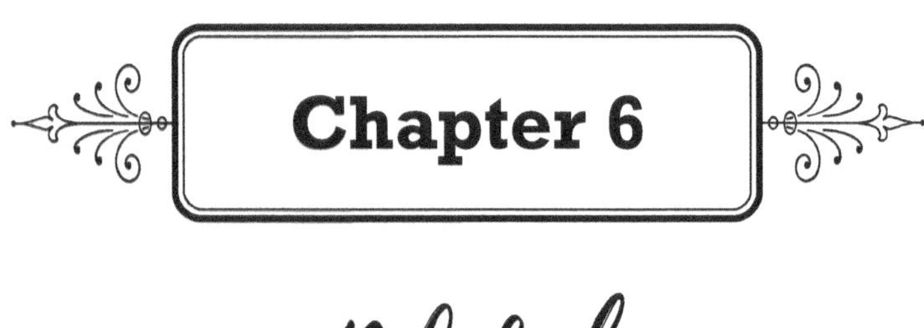

Rebekah

REBEKAH WAS THE DAUGHTER-IN-LAW OF Sarah. She was a young woman who had not even seen the man she had agreed to marry before she left on her journey for a new life. Before Rebekah left to start this new life, her family released her with their blessings on her and for her. You can read about this in scripture in Genesis 24.

> Then Isaac brought her into his mother Sarah's tent, and he took Rebekah, and she became his wife; and he loved her. Thus, Isaac was comforted after his mother's death. (Genesis 24:67)

Now God's promise would begin to unfold from the promise of numerous offspring coming from Isaac. Isaac was careful to fulfill God's law and marry a godly woman.

It would appear in the scriptures there was a fairly wide range of age differences between Isaac, who was forty years of age, to Rebekah, who was probably not even in her twenties. This man of God deeply loved his mother, but when his mother passed on, he had a wife to console him who had many characteristics of his mother. Rebekah was a kind, attractive woman who was wise and smart as well.

From the time of her marriage to the time of the birth of her twin boys, there appear to be twenty years. From the time of conception, there appeared to be a struggle going on within her womb between the babies. Isaac and Jacob were born totally with two different personalities. One son drew the attention of the father and the other the mother. Do you think this can cause trouble at any time when being favored is so evident? Let us look at the story and see if being a mom makes us do downright stupid things at times that can hurt a marriage, self, other kids, and mostly the heart of God.

As the boys grew, so did a seed planted by the devil. Rebekah was looking to cheat Esau out of his rightful birthright. Goodness me, this sweet lassie was a conniving woman willing to steal from her firstborn child for the next in line.

She may have honestly believed she was doing the right thing. The only thing is it was contrary to the will of God. Do you think she might have suffered consequences for what she put into place?

Rebekah was so intent on doing things her way she was willing to be sneaky with her husband to accomplish what she set out to do.

Ever done anything like she did, dear hearts? If we are honest, probably just about all of us have. Geniuses 27:12 continues through into the next few chapters.

They talked about how Isaac was going blind, and Rebekah used this to her advantage to set up the exchange of the blessing that was rightfully Esau's. Do you think that Esau could have felt really betrayed? Not just his brother but his mother also! Rebekah was willing to gamble a lot to get her own way for her baby boy.

When Jacob was concerned that a curse would be upon his head (Genesis 23:13), Mommy dearest said let the curse be upon me. Oh my, she was willing to risk a lot to get her own way. Do you think she might think she outsmarted God? Maybe she even thought that if she got the deed done, it would be done, and God would go, well, can't do anything about it now.

I think not. Because of Esau's anger and fear for Jacob's life, Rebekah had to send her precious son away. This son she loved above all else. Again, she had to protect him. I wonder if she thought that would solve the problem, out of sight, out of mind. The only thing is you can't hide from God, can you?

What price did Mommy pay for her actions? Well, she never solved the problem, and she never saw her son again. All of this is because she got ahead of God. I wonder if she felt it was worth it all in the end. The last years of her life would be with a husband who would more than likely have lost respect and trust in her and a son who felt less loved than his brother by his mother and a lot of things between her and God.

Her baby boy would become a man who would marry a woman that would cause grief for both of his parents. Some people may think that Rebekah was clever. I think she was conniving. If only Rebekah could have trusted her children's lives to be in God's hands as she did when she was chosen by God as Isaac's wife. Did God love her any less? No, but she paid a high price for her will, not Gods.

Chapter 7

If there ever was a bad woman, then this was Jezebel. Her husband was not much better. He was a rotten apple right to the core, but that gal Jezebel, well, she took the cake. 1 Kings 18:4 tells us how she was determined to kill off the Lord's prophets. It was never mentioned that she had anything to do with God. It was her spineless hubby that let God go and followed his wife's ways.

This woman was smart in a worldly way. She has an authoritative place. She had power, and she used it to her advantage. With every breath she took, she did wrong. She took the authoritative role away from her husband. Jezebel killed, lied, stole, destroyed, and got the people of the country to follow suit. This rotten woman is one I really do not want even to consider writing much about. Why have I even acknowledged her? Well, I'll tell you. Her husband was a Christian, and she was not. Hubby was also a weak man who did not lead his wife or his nation. His wife refused to listen, honor, and respect her husband. He betrayed his God, his country, and himself. His wife refused to listen to God even when she saw firsthand the power of the Lord. God was just and righteous for taking these two lives in a demeaning and demoralizing way. Without God and His grace, look at what we could become.

Chapter 8

HANNA WAS LOVED BY HER husband, and he showed favor to her. Even though Peninnah was married to the same man as Hanna and had his children, Peninnah was mean to Hanna.

In those times, if you could not bear children, you were an outcast. You were ridiculed, sneered at, belittled, and constantly laughed at and put down. Hanna had to endure this type of treatment for years. How hard this would have been, we could only imagine. I would think there would have been a fair bit of jealousy between these two women. Hanna had no children, and Peninnah didn't have love from her husband or shown that special favor.

The scriptures tell us in Samuel 1:6–7,

> And her adversary also provoked her because the Lord had shut up her womb. And as He did so year after year, when she went up to the house of the Lord, so she provoked her; she wept and did not eat.

Golly, Peninnah probably knew that this was the Lord's doings and really rubbed poor Hanna's nose in it. God continued year after year to do this. Year after year, Hanna had to endure this hardship. God had a reason for this hardship to be happening to Hanna. Let us take a look at what she finally said to God.

In the quietness of her own heart, she admits to God how she saw herself without God, only a handmaid one who, in light of His majesty, "I am nothing."

> And she vowed a vow and said, Oh Lord of hosts, if thou would indeed look on the affliction of thy handmaid, and remember me, and not forget thy handmaid, but wilt give unto thy handmaid a man child, then I will give him unto the Lord all the days of his life, and there shall no razor come upon his head. (1 Samuel 1:11)

She told God if you give me a child, I will give it back to you to use for Your glory. I will bring the child to the temple of God.

God knew Hanna's heart and knew she would keep her word to Him. Once she prayed in this manner, she then received the desire of her heart.

Let me remind you that we should not be praying so we can just get something but to be obedient to God because that is the one true desire of your heart.

Hanna was to take her son to the temple and hand him over after he was weaned. The age in those days for weaning was around the three-year mark. If it were me, I would have had that little boy on my hip and breast till he was eighteen, I'm thinking. Not Hanna, though she did what she told the Lord she would do. This was done with the full knowledge that she would not see her son but once a year. What a brave woman. On the other hand, she could have been praising God for the years she had with him and thankful for the once-a-year visit she had. It's the mindset that makes the difference in all our lives. God truly blessed her for her obedience and gave her seven more precious babies. None I believe as precious as her firstborn. For God wanted to use this boy, I believe He also wanted to use Hannah to teach us also, dear ladies. I think a person really needs to look at how long it took Hanna to get to the place where she would do what God wanted her to do right from the start.

Give me your life and that of your family is a cry of God today to all of us. We stand in His way when we look at only what we want. In fact, we don't look past our own desires because, many times, they are so strong. Are you willing to give it all up so God can be glorified through your sacrifice? Well, in another breath, we have Hanna's counterpart. She was a jealous wife, a person who was spiteful. It appears that at the time of the Jewish holidays that was a time that Hanna's nose was really rubbed into her being baron. Satan will always attack a person at their weak point, and jealousy was Peninnah's. It can, and it does, destroy you and so many relationships.

The abuse that Hanna suffered turned into years of blessings for her. She gave her first child to God for His glory, and God gave her seven more babies to cuddle and love. It is sad that Peninnah could not, no, would not look at Hanna as an excellent example of a servant of God. Prayer and obedience to God, with trusting in faith, was the life that Hanna led.

Chapter 9

The Queen of Sheba

First Kings 10:1–13

OH, BUT TO BE A woman with the heart of the queen of Sheba. What was it that she wanted in the worst way and went to great lengths to get it? She wanted to be wise. It makes you stop and ponder what you yourself have focused on more than anything in life.

The queen traveled many miles to see Solomon and learn. The queen had learned from others that Solomon got his wisdom from God. Knowing this, Queen Sheba spent time and money to prepare for her visit to the king. She was already smart enough to understand that she would need to be prepared to get the most from the king. In today's terms, I think she stroked his ego. She brought gifts of great wealth and importance and told him I really need to pick your brain; you are so smart. She had to be smart enough to let him know she really wanted him to coach her, and she really wanted his knowledge, not just him. She wanted the wisdom that Solomon had. She opened her heart to this, and he hers.

The queen concluded that all the people under Solomon's rule were very blessed to be there. She saw why God had chosen him to be there as ruler. The queen was wise in her own right. She continued to be in this man's good books by following his words of wisdom, well also sending presents throughout her life to reinforce her thankfulness for this wisdom. Making friends and not trying to overstep made this woman wise.

Chapter 10

The Woman at the Well

WE SEE IN THE NEW Testament the same type of woman, only in a different era. We do not know this dear woman's name, but she had a past that changed many people's lives who have read it. She appears to be the same as many women I have run across. Insecure and doesn't feel she could make it on her own, so she goes from one man to the other. I can't help but wonder what happened to her after she had a personal encounter with the Lord Jesus Christ. Did she become an evangelist or a preacher? When I get to heaven, I ask her.

> There cometh a woman of Samaria to draw water: Jesus saith unto her, give me to drink.
>
> (For his disciples were gone away unto the city to buy meat.)
>
> Then saith the woman of Samaria unto him, How is it that thou, being a Jew, askest drink of me, which am a woman of Samaria? for the Jews have no dealings with the Samaritans.
>
> Jesus answered and said unto her, If thou knewest the gift of God, and who it is that saith to thee, Give me to drink; thou wouldest have

asked of him, and he would have given thee living water.

The woman saith unto him, Sir, thou hast nothing to draw with, and the well is deep: from whence then hast thou that living water?

Art thou greater than our father Jacob, which gave us the well, and drank thereof himself, and his children, and his cattle?

Jesus answered and said unto her, Whosoever drinketh of this water shall thirst again:

But whosoever drinketh of the water that I shall give him shall never thirst; but the water that I shall give him shall be in him a well of water springing up into everlasting life.

The woman saith unto him, Sir, give me this water, that I thirst not, neither come hither to draw.

Jesus saith unto her, Go, call thy husband, and come hither.

The woman answered and said, I have no husband. Jesus said unto her, Thou hast well said, I have no husband:

For thou hast had five husbands; and he whom thou now hast is not thy husband: in that saidst thou truly.

The woman saith unto him, Sir, I perceive that thou art a prophet.

Our fathers worshipped in this mountain; and ye say, that in Jerusalem is the place where men ought to worship.

Jesus saith unto her, Woman, believe me, the hour cometh, when ye shall neither in this mountain, nor yet at Jerusalem, worship the Father.

Ye worship ye know not what: we know what we worship: for salvation is of the Jews.

But the hour cometh, and now is, when the true worshippers shall worship the Father in spirit and in truth: for the Father seeketh such to worship him.

God is a Spirit: and they that worship him must worship him in spirit and in truth.

The woman saith unto him, I know that Messias cometh, which is called Christ: when he is come, he will tell us all things.

Jesus saith unto her, I that speak unto thee am he.

And upon this came his disciples, and marvelled that he talked with the woman: yet no man said, What seekest thou? or, Why talkest thou with her?

The woman then left her water pot, and went her way into the city, and saith to the men,

Come, see a man, which told me all things that ever I did: is not this the Christ?

Then they went out of the city and came unto him. (John 4:7–30)

One thing is for sure. She was so excited, and she wanted as many as possible to come to the living waters. He changes us, heals us, and restores us when we open our hearts, soul, and mind to Him and His love, forgiveness, and mercy.

Chapter 11

THIS BOOK STARTS RIGHT OUT with these two women needing a go-between for carrying on an argument with one another. Paul asked a man to intervene. A man in the middle of women scrapping. I would not want to be him. To have an intervention was because it was affecting the church, it would appear it was becoming a catfight. There was no purring there but a whole lot of hissing. Verse 2 clearly says that they labored in the gospel, and their names were written in the Lamb's book of life.

So Christian women can attack one another. Who would have thought! How did they resolve this, you may wonder? In the same way, we should resolve any issue with the Word of God.

Verses 4–7, Rejoice in the Lord, always again, I say rejoice! Let everyone come to know your gentleness. The Lord is at hand. Be anxious for nothing, but in everything, by prayer and supplication with gratitude, make your requests known to God. And the peace of God, which passes all understanding, will protect your hearts and minds through Christ Jesus.

Encouraging words can affect the outcome of any dispute. I'm sorry and forgive me can cover a multitude of sins. I love these encouraging words in verse 13. I can do all things through Christ who strengthens me. After hearing these words, I really think these women of God had the courage and strength to forgive for their sake, the churches, and mostly for their Lord.

Chapter 12

Now this woman was found in an uncompromising position. She was caught with her skirt up to put it nicely. The horror of it all was it was a married man. This story prickles me because it acted like the man was so innocent that he never had to stand trial or before the people in shame.

Jesus was there at the hearing as well as the whole town. When she was brought in to face her accusations against her, they asked Jesus whether the punishment for someone like her should be stoning as prescribed by Mosaic Law. He ignores the accusers, bends, and writes on the ground as though He doesn't hear them. When the accusers continue to bait Him, He simply states the one that is without sin should cast the first stone. It didn't take long before they all left. Who could throw the stone in all reality? The only answer that is pure truth was JESUS. What Jesus did was ask the woman if anyone had condemned her. She said no one. He simply stated neither would condemn you: go and sin no more.

What a beautiful example this is to the love of Jesus no anger, no sneering, or finger-pointing. Her forgiveness was a done deal, and it was no more.

Dear women, this is so important. Do not let the world beat you up for your mistakes, and when they try, simply say my sins are covered by the blood. And please, dear ladies, don't whip yourselves but live under the grace of the blood and choose to forgive yourselves.

There are women throughout the Bible who didn't do anything wrong but were treated as though they did. I know many of us have had this happen. But before I close the pages, I want to name one from the old and one from the new.

Hanna
First Samuel

In the Old Testament, we have Hanna. You can read about it in 1 Samuel. She prayed for years to have a child. Looking into history, it appears to be nineteen years plus.

This precious woman was a mockery because she was a baron. Women like her would not even go to get water at the well at the same time as the gathering of the women did. She was the laughing-stock of the women. What a burden she had to pay for not being able to conceive.

She then goes to the temple, and she is praying to the Lord. Scripture states she was in bitterness of soul and prayed unto the Lord and wept sore. Then along comes the priest, who accuses her and chastises her for being drunk. It doesn't look like she got much of a break in life.

Oh, but the grace of God. God gave her the desires of her heart. She gave her precious son back to be used for God, and God blessed her with seven more children. That's a bit more than double for her trouble, do I think.

Mary

Talked about in various books of the Bible—the mother of our Lord Jesus Christ, a young woman of fourteen who was promised in marriage to Joseph. She was never mentioned before except to hear the angel of the Lord tell her she was going to have the son of GOD. She did not hesitate for a moment but said, "Be it unto me." In those times, she should have been stoned for being pregnant outside the marriage bed. Her future hubby heard from the Lord, and he continued with the marriage. She would have been talked about if not in front of her, at least behind the doors or the gatherings of the women. She risked it all to be obedient to her calling.

I think we pretty well all know the outcome of that experience. You, dear ladies, may be talked about, lied about, and treated badly, but I am telling you, You are the delight of the Lord, and He says, you are beautifully and wonderfully made. When you are feeling less, than let those words sink into your spirit and walk in them.

I pray a blessing on all you lovely ladies that have taken the time to read the words on the pages. May each of you be blessed in your going out and your coming in and your in between. May you see your value as God sees them every moment of every day of the rest of your lives, in Jesus's name; Amen and Amen.

Sue Doble-Dumoulin is a wife to her sweetheart, Gil Dumoulin—a mother to seven children, a Nana to twenty-five grandchildren, including step-grandchildren, and a GG to eleven great-grandchildren. Sue loves her family and all that comes into her life, even for a season.

Sue is what some people would call a jack of all trades. She was a pioneer. Fostered for seventeen years, having fifty-four children grace her home—some she adopted.

Sue put her hand to anything that needed to be done, whether it be building the home, plumbing, electrical, and so much more. She made all her food from scratch, including homemade bread and goodies. Sue canned every type of food she could. She sewed outfits and quilts.

There was one item she had to give up in the tool department when she married Gil, which was her chainsaw. She loves writing, this being her second book. She loves each day and rejoices in it. Sue feels at seventy-five, her life has just truly begun.